DISCOVERING AND DEVELOPING A SECRET LIFE OF PRAYER

DAVID LEE MARTIN

—

INTRODUCTION

TO MY FELLOW TRAVELERS

> "Not that I have already attained, or am already perfected; but I press on, that I may lay hold of that for which Christ Jesus has also laid hold of me."
>
> — PHILIPPIANS 3:12 NKJV

This book is written to fellow travelers. To other children looking with wonder at the stars above, awed by what our Papa in Heaven has invited us to enjoy. It is not written with a heart that says, "I've arrived and have so much to say." Instead it is written with an ear open to the Father's leading, looking daily to go deeper and to share that journey with others.

I hope it is a blessing to you, and opens new streams of grace within your heart.

David

JOIN THE PRAYER PRINCIPLES NEWSLETTER...

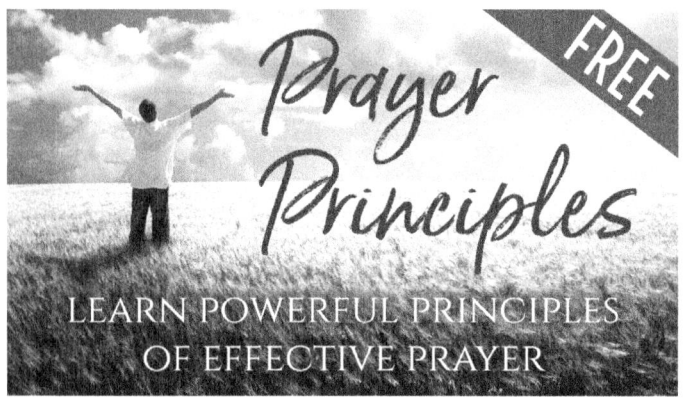

Go to JesusChrist.uk to subscribe

The Prayer Principles Teaching Series is a regular bite-size teaching newsletter designed to equip you to pray more effectively, and to know God in a deeper and more satisfying way.

You will **learn spiritual keys and practical principles** that you can actually use in your own passionate pursuit of God and His purpose for your life. The easy-to-digest lessons are designed to drive your heart to delight in prayer like never before.

As well as free books, videos & anointed training in proven pathways to the Father's presence you will receive teaching on…

• The Privilege of Prayer

• The Spirit of Prayer

• Passion and Prayer

• Different Kinds of Prayer

• Praying in the Spirit

• Speaking In Tongues

• Inspiring stories of answered prayer

• United Prayer

• Tabernacle or Temple Prayer

• Praying the Lord's Prayer

• Fasting and Prayer

• The Prayer of Faith

• Working and Walking with God in Prayer

• Deepening Your Relationship With God Through Prayer

• New resources created to build your spirit and stir your passion for God

…and much, much more.

Join thousands of fellow prayer warriors who are already taking this journey...

Subscribe at JesusChrist.uk

HIDDEN PRAYER

O, LET THE PLACE OF SECRET PRAYER
BECOME TO ME THE MOST BELOVED
SPOT ON EARTH. — ANDREW MURRAY

Hidden prayer. No subject is so close to my heart! In fact, only the heart can truly comprehend the marvelous opportunity we have been given. Cultivating a secret life of prayer is the great quest of every believer.

The richness and wonder of knowing God, and the deepening friendship we can enjoy with Him, captivates the heart of Jesus followers everywhere. It is the journey we all take and rejoice that we never arrive. There is always more to discover!

It does not take long to realize that the reward of secret prayer is in itself. We begin by bringing our requests but soon realize that God answers with Himself. His presence and knowing and walking in Him is answer enough. "Seek first," He said, "and

1

everything else will be added" (Matthew 6:33). The focus soon shifts from the things we want to add, to the satisfaction of seeking and finding greater depths of God to enjoy.

I have spent literally thousands of hours secretly praying, and even now I crave to go to a deeper place in prayer. Hunger begets hunger and nothing but His presence can satisfy a heart that has tasted His exquisite goodness.

My purpose in writing this book however is not to talk about my prayer life. I want to feed into yours. I want to affirm and celebrate your desire to know God. I want to provoke you to pursuit, and woo you to put aside other things and let Heaven fill your thoughts.

Without question, the very fact that you are reading this book tells me that you share my hunger for more of God. The mystery of knowing God has captured your heart and is drawing you deeper.

The place that such hunger finds relief is behind the door, closed off from the world, and steeped in a growing love-infused relationship with your Papa in heaven.

The invitation has been extended to you to come inside. You have said, "Yes, Lord", and now by His grace He will put keys into your hand that will usher you into greater depths.

Let's close the door on excuses and shun the world's estimation of what's worthy of our energies, and set aside time to secretly seek. When you do, rewards beyond compare will be yours.

REWARD

Rarely do people do anything without some kind of reward in mind. Our Papa's invitation to prayer comes with a promise. He is not asking us to pray as a dry duty, or for His benefit; it is entirely for ours, and an opportunity we don't want to miss.

We don't have to pray. We get to pray!

We don't have to read the Bible. We get to read the Bible!

We don't have to worship. We get to worship!

The privilege is all ours. What an amazing opportunity! What a miracle God has wrought through Christ that ushers us into freedom and friendship with the Almighty God.

One of my favorite portions of Scripture is of course the Sermon on the Mount. What a concentrated dose of truth Jesus provides from the hill top! In it He covers a whole host of subjects, but a secret life of prayer and unseen devotion are part of that.

He tells the assembled crowd to close the door on the world and pray secretly to a loving Father, and that God, who sees in secret, will surely hear and reward abundantly and openly.

Elsewhere in Scripture we are told again and again that God rewards those who earnestly and diligently seek him (Hebrews 11:6).

> "But without faith it is impossible to please *and* be satisfactory to Him. For whoever would come near to God must [necessarily] believe that God exists and that He is the rewarder of those who earnestly *and* diligently seek Him [out]."
>
> — HEBREWS 11:6 AMPLIFIED

With such incredible promises on the table, and absolute certainty of reward for secret seeking, what holds you back from making this a top priority in your life?

DON'T STAY ON THE SURFACE, GO TO THE DEPTHS

TO DESIRE REVIVAL... AND AT THE SAME TIME TO NEGLECT (PERSONAL) PRAYER AND DEVOTION IS TO WISH ONE WAY AND WALK ANOTHER. — A.W. TOZER

The Bible speaks about deep calling unto deep.

"Deep calls to deep at the sound of Your waterfalls; All Your breakers and Your waves have rolled over me."

— PSALMS 42:7 NAS95

The deep in God is calling to the deep places in you. God is a Spirit and to engage with Him personally requires that your spirit reach out.

"God is a Spirit: and they that worship him must worship him in spirit and in truth."

— JOHN 3:5; 4:24 KJV

Just parroting prayers is not really praying it all. It may have some benefit in comforting the soul, but it is not prayer in the truest sense of the word.

The trouble is that many believers, sincere followers of Jesus, remain in the surface waters when it comes to prayer. They live lives that are outwardly active in service to God, but behind the scenes their prayer lives are pretty anemic.

What does your life of worship and prayer look like? Is it like the iceberg in this picture, or do we have it the other way around, where the weight of our life is played out in public with only a small portion of our resources and energies offered secretly before the Father?

I encourage you, wherever you are on the journey right now, not to be condemned or come down on yourself. Papa is waiting eagerly to receive you. The Holy Spirit is here to help you pray!

> "So too the [Holy] Spirit comes to our aid and bears us up in our weakness; for we do not know what prayer to offer nor how to offer it worthily as we ought, but the Spirit Himself goes to meet our supplication and pleads in our behalf with unspeakable yearnings and groanings too deep for utterance."
>
> — ROMANS 8:26 AMPLIFIED

There is so much more that we could say about this Scripture, but for now just know this - God is more interested in you developing a deep, rich experience of Himself than you are! His hunger for your

8

fellowship is equal to and more than your hunger to know Him.

That means that there are four willing participants in this wild adventure - Father, Son, Holy Spirit and you!

Believe not only that such depths are open, but that they have been made available to you.

As you prioritize prayer you will be amazed at the intimate wonders God will lead you into.

DESIRE

PRAYER SHOULD NOT BE REGARDED AS
A DUTY WHICH MUST BE PERFORMED,
BUT RATHER AS A PRIVILEGE TO BE
ENJOYED, A RARE DELIGHT THAT IS
ALWAYS REVEALING SOME NEW
BEAUTY. — E.M. BOUNDS

D esire is the beginning of any venture of the spirit.

The Bible tells us that God plants His desires in our heart.

> "Delight thyself also in the LORD; and he shall give thee the desires of thine heart."
>
> — PSALMS 37:4 KJV

I believe that the most fundamental of these desires, and one that He plants deeply in every born-again believer, is the desire to know Him. Really know Him.

Religion is such a pale and pathetic pastiche of what's really possible. Jesus never prescribed to a life of religious drudgery. If anything, he was violently opposed to any religious activity that was not born of the spirit. He spoke about the outer man and the inner man, and how even seemingly zealous religious activity could cloak a heart of dead obedience to rules, regulations and ultimately self-serving pride.

Solomon's treatise on the futility of life without God has a most wonderful insight:

> "He has made everything beautiful in its time. He also has planted eternity in men's hearts *and* minds [a divinely implanted sense of a purpose working through the ages which nothing under the sun but God alone can satisfy]…"
>
> — ECCLESIASTES 3:11 AMPLIFIED

Friend, there is something within you that cries out every moment like a child for its mother. It is the deepest, most profoundly elemental need of the human heart - to know and be known by God.

At a base level it's the cry for love.

We chase it here. Search for it there. All the while God is waiting, ready to fulfil and meet that inherent spirit-driven need for closeness and community.

Sex cannot satisfy. Riches fall far short. Success is short lived and empty in comparison. Even the best of human relationships leave an unspoken yearning gnawing away on the inside.

It is the desire for God.

Moving from the raw passion to practical outworking, there are some keys that can act as desire stirrers, stoking the fire of your heart to action. When the fires burn bright on the inside, it becomes easy to pray. The man or woman on fire is always on the lookout for another moment to connect with heaven.

Pastor Paul Y Cho, a man of mountain top prayer if ever there was one, pointed out in his book, *Prayer - Key To Revival*, the importance of developing real desire in the heart before praying. Deep desire precedes deep intercession, and is an essential ingredient to both the quality and longevity of our prayers.

Jesus too spoke about coming to God and asking for "whatsoever we desire in our heart":

> "Therefore I say unto you, What things soever ye desire, when ye pray, believe that ye receive *them*, and ye shall have *them*."

> — MARK 11:24 KJV

Notice that prayer is preceded by desire.

Building this desire is essential if you want to persevere long enough to establish yourself a place in the spirit that you can call your own. A secret place, sculpted together with the Holy Spirit and into which you can step at any moment and meet with Him.

The very best way I have found to accomplish this desire building exercise is to become acutely aware of the benefits of a secret life with God.

We have already looked at reward. There is nothing wrong with being motivated by reward. God promises it for a reason. He knows that we will not pursue something that offers minimal benefits. People do not rise early and work late for their employer because of the goodness of their hearts. They do it for reward! They know that at the end of the week, or the month, or the year, they will be recognized and recompensed for their time and effort.

Let me tell you, the rewards of secret seeking are far greater than any payout the world can offer.

Take the Bible and comb it diligently for all of the promises that surround a life of prayer and secret devotion to the one true God. Underline them, write them down, speak them out in the first person…

"The effective, fervent prayers that I pray avail much, and make tremendous power available…"

"I seek God secretly and He rewards me openly…"

"I ask for whatsoever things I desire, believing that I receive them, and my Father in Heaven hears and gives to me those things that I have desired."

"Through knowing Him, and becoming ever more intimately acquainted with Jesus, I am abundantly supplied with all things that pertain to life and godliness."

You get the idea.

Begin to solidify the pictures you have on the inside of a vibrant life of prayer and fellowship with God. Banish lies that paint a grey, uninviting canvas of duty and drudgery, or an anemic atmosphere of one way conversation filled with religious platitudes. These are not the images that the Bible gives us of life with God. They are lies and should be treated with the disdain they deserve.

Knowing God and becoming acquainted with the trinity - a rich and heroic fellowship of the heart - is the most passionate, personal and powerful privilege we will ever enjoy!

Meditate on the benefits of being in His presence daily, and hearing His direction at every junction of life. Consider the awesome implications of being a true man or woman of prayer who carries the yoke-destroying anointing of the Holy Spirit wherever you walk.

As the picture builds day-by-day, line-upon-line, layer-upon-layer, little-by-little, the benefits of pursuit will quickly be perceived to outweigh the comforts of passivity. Passion will rise and you will begin to actively seek out places and people who can feed into and nourish your growing desire to know God in an intimate way.

When we grasp the benefits of something, the heart becomes willing to lay aside its protestations and excuses and apply itself to something we otherwise often find is in short supply - discipline.

DISCIPLINE

THE GREAT PEOPLE OF THE EARTH
TODAY ARE THE PEOPLE WHO PRAY,
(NOT) THOSE WHO TALK ABOUT
PRAYER. — S.D.GORDON

D iscipline. It's a subject that is rarely spoken of nowadays, even in Christian circles. The word 'disciple' literally means "disciplined one". Sadly, despite being the disciplined ones of Jesus, the tendency is still to lean to our comforts, not rock the boat, and certainly not to push ourselves beyond the point that others might call fanatical.

It is also worth noting here that the Secret Place of Prayer is not talking about a physical closet or environment, it is a place in the spirit. The secret place is a spiritual territory. It belongs to you, it was made for you, and no one else can rightfully and legitimately occupy the space that Papa reserved for your own unique relationship to flourish - but you must nevertheless occupy it.

Through consistent fervent action in the spirit we establish our place in the heavens. It is in truth our natural environment, and it is only here that we rediscover who we really are and what we were made for.

That process takes discipline, especially at the front end when we are first reclaiming our God-given inheritance.

It is also important to remember that discipline is not the end-game. It is simply a tool we use to get us to our final destination.

You don't become a skilled workman in the natural without significant discipline being applied in a particular direction. Equally, you cannot be skillful in the spiritual realm if you do not diligently apply yourself to learn the disciplines of prayer and understand the technologies that God has put in place to accomplish His will in the spiritual world.

That is one reason why the *work* needs to be preceded by the *want*. Discipline follows desire. Desire is like the gas in the tank that then propels the vehicle to its destination. Discipline is the vehicle we need to strap ourselves into if we want to reach the fruition of our secret pursuit - a place called Delight.

I'm not going to pretend it's easy to carve out a space in the heavenlies to pray. It's not. There is such resistance to prayer on all levels, and the devil especially seeks to thwart the development of a powerful praying man or woman.

Samuel Chadwick wrote:

"The one concern of the devil is to keep the saints from praying. He fears nothing from prayer-less studies, prayer-less work, prayer-less religion. He laughs at our toil, mocks at our wisdom, but trembles when we pray."

How true this is. If the devil can't distract us with sin he will keep us busy like saints. Anything, so long as we don't have time, focus or energy to pray!

A praying person is a powerful person. A praying church is a powerful church. A church on its knees is one that stands strong in the heavens. The thing is, a praying church is made up of praying people.

It begins in the closet. Hidden away from others a man or woman is forged by God into a mighty weapon.

THE GREATEST ENEMY OF PRIVATE PRAYER

WHILE WE ARE LOOKING AT GOD WE DO NOT SEE OURSELVES — BLESSED RIDDANCE. — A.W. TOZER

The greatest enemy of private prayer and the development of a strong life of fellowship away from prying eyes is not Satan.

The greatest enemy is yourself.

Your untamed flesh nature will buck and fight you every step of the way. It will seek to preserve its place of primacy and push you to fill your hours with pleasurable distractions. Especially pernicious ones and favorites of the modern untamed soul are entertainment (the Facebook and Netflix syndrome) and busyness, where we suddenly feel the urge to wash the dishes or do the ironing despite hating those chores at any other moment of the day!

Prayer dislodges the grip the world has upon us.

The crazy thing is that our flesh nature, left to its own devices, welcomes and feeds the hold and claims that the world has upon us.

When we pray, alone and with fervency, our spirit (the real person on the inside) takes ascendency. Our being begins to come into clear alignment with the will and purpose of God.

As we break into those purposes, we break away from the grip of the world and the flesh.

The problem that many of us face is that this process takes discipline.

It is like breaking a horse. The flesh nature wants to remain in charge. It does not want to be saddled and subservient to the spirit. That's why there is such conflict in the establishment of a strong personal prayer life.

We face resistance from outside, but there is often agreement within our own soul with those distractions, excuses and barriers that are erected to keep us in the natural and as far away from the spirit as is possible.

You are a spirit, created in the image of God. We dwell in flesh and blood bodies but the essence of a human being cannot be boiled down to a neat pile of carbon atoms and other elements.

God is a Spirit.

Those who worship Him must do so in spirit and in truth:

> "God is a Spirit (a spiritual Being) and those who worship Him must worship *Him* in spirit and in truth (reality)."
>
> — JOHN 4:24 AMPLIFIED

The hosts of hell and distractions of the world will conspire to keep you out of the spirit. The devil knows that once you are there, you are alive and dangerous to his kingdom of lies. Your flesh will know that it can no longer dangle a slice of pizza in your face and derail your call to Kingdom business.

Your spirit is like a fish out of water in this dry and barren world. The (super) natural environment you were designed to swim in is the spiritual realm. Once there, having tasted just how amazingly good our Papa and His Spirit are, you are spoiled for anything else.

Breaking the Horse

Let's go back to the picture of our flesh nature as an unbroken horse.

I am no horseman so anyone with even a meager knowledge of the actual process will need to forgive me. I assume that there are comparisons with breaking the grip of our flesh over our lives.

No wild horse in its right mind wants to be tamed. It wants to run at will across the plains, unharnessed and free to twist and turn in whatever direction it pleases. It is strong, well fed and muscular, and is used to being its own master.

Our flesh in many ways is just like that horse.

It has been given all the liberty it wants to run in whatever direction it chooses.

Our flesh has been fed and pampered and yielded to for so many years that it will not buckle without a fight. The flesh wants to stay in control, determine where and when you move (usually to the kitchen or the armchair) and kicks violently against anything that suggests it should surrender its place and be saddled for purposeful action in any other realm than its own.

For me, the breaking process began when I acted on the desire I spoke about in the previous chapters. I knew for certain that there was treasure on the other side of this journey into the spirit, but had no clue how to even begin getting there.

My flesh fussed and fought me all the way. My mind would run rampant like an untamed foal in every direction other than toward God.

My corral was my bedroom.

Before I relate my early prayer history, I want to be clear that I do not believe that this is necessary for everyone. The process of breaking though and becoming more aware of spiritual things will be different for each one of us. I do believe however that a process of moving from being dominated by our natural man toward spiritual awareness and strength is inescapable and every disciple will go through it in their own unique way.

In order to instigate the breaking process I emptied my bedroom of everything that could take my attention away from the important task at hand - prayer. With only my bed as company, I locked myself inside.

I then told myself, out loud like a parent to an annoying child, that I would be there for the next hour, sometimes two, so I may as well get with the plan and pray.

I did this day after day, before and/or after work.

I remember well the first few times, shouting out to God, "God, here I am. I have no idea how to pray or even begin to speak with You, but I'm here. Help me!"

"Help me!"

A perennial prayer that never grows old.

And He did.

Gradually my guard came down, the stubborn resolve of my soulish flesh nature to stay in control gave way, and a trickle of spiritual life began to bubble up from my spirit.

Jesus spoke of it this way:

> "Those who drink the water I give will never be thirsty again. It becomes a fresh, bubbling spring within them, giving them eternal life."
>
> — JOHN 4:14 NLT

There were many times during that season I had no words to fill the hours. I would pace the floor simply saying, "God, teach me to pray." "God, help me to know You." "God, I want to know how to seek You."

Little by little the discipline began to give way to something far more powerful.

As life bubbled up from my inner man, and I embraced the process and yielded to the utterances of heaven coming up from within my spirit, the need for discipline dissipated.

It was like the horse no longer needed a harness to force or coerce it into obedience. A gentle tap was enough to turn its head.

Discipline gave way to delight.

DELIGHT

"Delight yourself also in the Lord, and He will give you the desires *and* secret petitions of your heart."

— PSALMS 37:4 AMPLIFIED

You have now been ushered into the realm of powerful personal prayer. It is a place called *delight*.

Once you have broken through the resistance, prayer and private devotion quickly become your place of refuge. It is the flourishing oasis we flee to in an otherwise barren landscape.

You no longer need to convince yourself of the

benefits of secret seeking. Duty is a word that simply is not found in our new dictionary.

Secret prayer is the joy of the heart, because it brings us face-to-face with our Savior and into the presence of our Beloved.

Even in human relations, truly knowing someone in an intimate manner, as Adam *knew* his wife (Genesis 4:1), happens in private. The deepest connections are not ones that happen in public.

The more intimate the melding of spirits, the more private and secret the environment needs to be. It is the same in prayer.

Folks talk about praying in transit, scattershot prayers while they go about their other important daily business (busy-ness may be a better description for much of the activity we term otherwise), but let's get real. How many of you husbands and wives make love while you drive, or when you are shopping in the mall? The swirl of the world is not the place of intimacy.

Your desire and delight in one another willingly drives you behind closed doors where nakedness is normal and shame is a stranger.

So it is in God's perfect presence. Intimate moments of deep communion are found most often deep in the secret place of prayer. The gentle whispers of love saved for you alone are reserved for that place. They are not public announcements; they are the sweet utterances of lovers embraced.

The heart is satisfied only in relationship, and craves more than mere friendship when it finally finds its soul mate. Papa wants to speak intimately with you, but we must position ourselves appropriately to hear His most confidential and close communications. One of my favorite verses (another one - I have many!) speaks of Moses and his relationship with the Father:

 "There I will meet with you and, from above the mercy seat, from between the two cherubim that are upon the ark of the Testimony, I will speak intimately with you…"

— EXODUS 25:22 AMPLIFIED

Deep inside the tabernacle, beyond the gaze of the world, and overshadowed by angel wings, Moses and his God spoke intimately.

Papa speaks intimately today. But only to those who venture deep enough behind the veil to listen.

The wonderful thing about moving beyond discipline as the driver for your time alone with God is that the habit now formed makes stepping between natural and supernatural almost seamless. Whereas at one time it would take me substantial time to move through the veil, it is now almost instantaneous. My spirit is primed for prayer. Not only that, I do not have to stir myself to pray; it is pushing up from the everlasting well within my heart every moment of the day.

God is calling you inside. He is whispering your name right now, gently and affectionately inviting you deeper.

Will you meet with Him and be melted in His presence?

I hope so.

THE SECRET PLACE

TRUE PRAYER IS NEITHER A MERE
MENTAL EXERCISE NOR A VOCAL
PERFORMANCE. IT IS FAR DEEPER THAN
THAT - IT IS SPIRITUAL TRANSACTION
WITH THE CREATOR OF HEAVEN AND
EARTH. — CHARLES SPURGEON

T he 'secret place' is a term derived from the teachings of Jesus commonly referred to as the Sermon on the Mount.

Speaking to the crowds, and later and in more depth to his disciples, Jesus comes at the whole realm of personal prayer in this way:

> "But thou, when thou prayest, enter into thy closet, and when thou hast shut thy door, pray to thy Father which is in secret; and thy Father which seeth in secret shall reward thee openly."

> — MATTHEW 6:5–6 KJV

There are a couple of things here worth noting. Prayer is a given. Not "if" you pray, but "when" you pray. Secondly, prayer, when approached with a right heart, is rewarded! There are incalculable benefits for the praying saint that so many sincere Christians fail to appropriate.

Jesus speaks of coming into our closet, a secret place where the doors are shut on the clamor of the world. The thing to remember in all of this, however, and indeed any time we come to the realm of prayer, is that God is a Spirit.

Your secret place is in reality a place in the spirit realm where you engage in intimate communion and partnership with God. It is something that you establish through exercising your spirit and developing your awareness of God and His realm of operation and existence.

Too many people, sincere believers even, waste their time merely *saying* prayers. There is a world of difference between just saying our prayers, and really entering into the spirit of prayer and praying from the heart. Spirit to Spirit prayer lifts us out of the natural world and into an awareness of God's reality and presence that is tangible and transformative.

I liken the establishment of the secret place to

someone going into wild untamed country and cultivating the land. We remove hindrances and obstacles to fruitfulness. Squatters are evicted, and the land is cultivated. We establish a strong presence on that plot of spiritual land and call it our own. There is a real sense of possession, a personal promised land in the spirit. An awareness of God's reality permeates this special place of encounter.

As you give yourself to prayer you become given to prayer, if that makes sense. Like any addiction, the more we yield to something the greater its grip becomes upon us, and the less resistance there remains within us when the desire comes calling to be satisfied.

More often than not this is ascribed to bad habits and sinful pursuits, but the same is true of Godly activities.

Paul speaks of this in the book of Romans:

> "Likewise reckon ye also yourselves to be dead indeed unto sin, but alive unto God through Jesus Christ our Lord. Let not sin therefore reign in your mortal body, that ye should obey it in the lusts thereof. **Neither yield ye your members as instruments of**

unrighteousness unto sin: but yield yourselves unto God, as those that are alive from the dead, and your members as instruments of righteousness unto God. For sin shall not have dominion over you: for ye are not under the law, but under grace. What then? Shall we sin, because we are not under the law, but under grace? God forbid. **Know ye not, that to whom ye yield yourselves servants to obey, his servants ye are to whom ye obey**; whether of sin unto death, or of obedience unto righteousness?"

— ROMANS 6:11–16 KJV

We become servants to the thing we yield ourselves to - flesh or spirit. Consistently seeking out and yielding to the spirit of prayer makes us prone to pray. We are given to it, in the same way one might say of a drunkard that they are 'given' to alcohol. In the case of the alcoholic, all the barriers have come down and no inner fight remains against the next glass or bottle. So it is with the praying man or woman. You grow so accustomed to yielding when the Spirit taps your shoulder or whispers to your heart that no resistance prevents you from flowing right into partnering right then and there with the Holy Ghost.

And believe me, there is resistance to prayer on every side. The devil hates prayer like a plague, but the greatest battle is within.

Our soul and flesh, and by that I mean our unsanctified thoughts, feelings, desires and wilful selfishness, has so often been yielded to over the years that it is reluctant to give up control. Our flesh kicks and screams at the discomfort of stepping into the unknown. Our mind protests at every turn that we are "just making it up" or that "prayer is pointless". Or on the other side of that same coin, it may seek to retain control by standardizing and ritualizing prayer so it becomes mechanical and lifeless.

Jesus spoke of how the lifeblood of spirituality is drained dry by dead traditions:

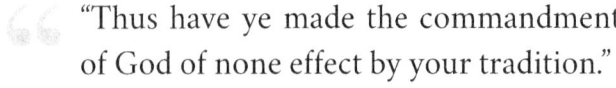

"Thus have ye made the commandment of God of none effect by your tradition."

— MATTHEW 15:6 KJV

There is a wrestling within us as flesh-enveloped and broken beings that actively kicks against the things of the Spirit. Romans 8 describes the conflict well.

> "Because the carnal mind is enmity against God: for it is not subject to the law of God, neither indeed can be. So then they that are in the flesh cannot please God. But ye are not in the flesh, but in the Spirit, if so be that the Spirit of God dwell in you."
>
> — ROMANS 8:6–9 KJV

The practice of prayer, especially private prayer and praying in tongues, challenges the authority of our flesh, and calls forward our spirit to engage with God. Your sanctified spirit (the real you!) rises and begins to take control, and especially in the early stages of developing a stronger prayer life, our soul and flesh do all they can to hinder it. I have no doubt that you have all experienced the gentle tug of the Holy Ghost to the place of prayer, and as if from nowhere the almost irresistible urge to make another cup of coffee or clean that cobweb from the corner (where it has remained undisturbed for several months) grips us with insistent urgency.

The question is, what do you do in that instant? To

whom do you yield? As you make your choice the power of either the flesh or the spirit is strengthened and the other diminished in your life.

The point I am making here is that a strong secret prayer life, and establishing yourself as a force to be reckoned with in the spiritual realm, is not something that is built over night. It is developed day-by-day, choice-by-choice, until it becomes habitual in the very best sense of the word. The junction of decision becomes less congested with other demands, and our heart easily tips into praying with little protest from either the devil (who knows he is defeated) or your own flesh.

TO HAVE GOD SPEAK TO THE HEART IS
A MAJESTIC EXPERIENCE, AN
EXPERIENCE THAT PEOPLE MAY MISS IF
THEY MONOPOLIZE THE
CONVERSATION AND NEVER PAUSE TO
HEAR GOD'S RESPONSES. — CHARLES
STANLEY

The secret life is made of daily communion. Consistency is a major ingredient in the deepening walk you enjoy with God's Holy Spirit.

I liken it in one way to the manna that fell from heaven each day in the wilderness to feed the hunger of the Israelites.

Manna actually means "what is it?"

There was a mystery here that left the people of God thankful but scratching their heads. Each day, this mysterious honey bread would fall like snow from heaven, caking the ground, and was meant to sustain them for the day. If the manna was kept overnight it rotted. Yesterday's manna, if it was not gathered and consumed then and there, was no longer available. Each day brought its own "what is it" for the people to eat.

God has bread to share with you each day. It is the bread of His Word. We are sustained and satisfied not with yesterday's word. We need a new word for every day.

I guess this is where my FOMO kicks in. That's a modern acronym that I learned recently. It means Fear Of Missing Out. For most in our infotainment saturated culture their FOMO drives to check their phone 140 times a day - for people like you, who are not of this world - it drives you to your prayer closet for another dose of the Ghost.

I don't want to miss out in what God wants to say today, because I know it won't be available to me again tomorrow. Tomorrow has its own word to share.

I want to faithfully gather up words in my ears each day, and consume them. I want them to form me over time into a true man of God. Someone who truly knows his Father.

Real life is not made up of banquets. Most days may

be unimpressive, meat and two veg days. Every so often a special occasion presents us with a meal that blows our socks off, but that is not the norm. We don't live on party food.

So it is in the spirit. Sometimes God has prepared a stunning encounter. Those days are so glorious. Literally life-changing. We most certainly don't want to miss those! Thing is, the invitations are not sent before the event. We never know when we step into our secret place what God has prepared for that day. It could be the very moment He has predestined to visit you in a way that will change the world forever. What if on that day you decide a couple hours more sleep, or another episode of your favorite TV serial is more appealing?

I do not want to sow fear in your heart, just awaken you to the possibility that seeking God should be a priority every day. Not for His benefit but for yours.

And also to encourage you that the many meat and two veg days that sandwich those mountain top moments are just as miraculous and form the substance of a life deeply engaged with Heaven. Like a marriage built on moment-by-moment knowing of one another, so our walk with divinity is often built in the everyday interactions that otherwise look mundane.

Each day God has a unique, never to be repeated "what is it?" moment to share with you. Bread from heaven.

Every day is an opportunity to hear Him speak to your heart, and those words build over time to develop a rich, rooted, intimate friendship of deep trust and love.

Don't miss your manna.

GOD SHAPES THE WORLD BY PRAYER.
THE MORE PRAYING THERE IS IN THE
WORLD THE BETTER THE WORLD WILL
BE, THE MIGHTIER THE FORCES
AGAINST EVIL. — E M BOUNDS

"We have history, Lord."

Those are the words that came out of my mouth a few mornings ago whilst praying. They were profound to my ears!

It was one of those days when prayer was a struggle. My heart was in knots over something and the flow was stifled. But I remembered that I knew my God. I remembered that He is faithful. But most of all, I remembered that we are friends. We have history!

The writers of the Bible remembered this too in their relationship with Papa. Psalms especially is filled with urgent remembrance of God's Word and work in the lives of His people. When times were hard and God seemed distant, a history of surety securely anchored the people's prayers. The past acted as a bridge to the present, bringing the heart back into the Presence.

It felt good to know that God and I had walked a good long mile or two together. Some leaping across the peaks, others crawling through the valley, but all in His care and with His direction.

The thing is, history is not built on tomorrows. It is built on today. Each day spent seeking. Each hour given to know Him better. All add up over time to a life lived in God's presence. We build a rich and textured history that no circumstance can steal.

Even if this present moment is fraught with confusion or disappointment. Even if you feel like the most faithless person on the planet. History gives assurance.

Your history with God, that relationship that endures and has put down deep roots, is being built today.

Can you look back and recall His closeness? Can you bring to mind His many words, spoken personally to your heart over the years that you have walked together?

Each day passed over with the prayer closet

untouched is another day lost in this rich adventure that your Papa wants to share with you.

Your life is made up of days. And how you spend your days determines your destiny and its fruit. If spiritual intimacy and relationship with God is something you crave, it will not come prepackaged in some kind of spirit-filled microwave meal. It cannot be ordered and delivered next day on Amazon.

Your history, whether at its just budding with its first tender stalks or maturing through the years, is built with the hours you have been blessed with this day.

And once that history is built and building you have an abundant stock of remembrance that sets you up for victory and peace whatever comes your way. You will be able to recall the times He brought you through. The times He provided against the odds. The times He carried you beyond yourself and your sense of inadequacy and came through on your behalf.

Every day of fellowship builds upon those before, and every battle fought and won makes you stronger, not because of the winning so much as the deeper place you were forced to connect with heaven in order to find the necessary grace to overcome. Because we must dig beyond our experience and reach for more of His comfort and power in trying situations, we come out the other side knowing more of Him. That, to me, is the true reward of testing. Even seeming failures can become points of rich blessing because in and through them we have been driven deeper into the Father's embrace. My most challenging times in life have taught me the hard way that I must not seek affirmation or a sense of worth from what I do or from other people. Sometimes I believe that the Father, jealous for our affections, removes the crutches that prop up our ego in order to usher us deeper into our true identity in Him. These are not necessarily experiences I invite, but when they present themselves I do my very best to see them as an opportunity to know the Godhead in a new way, and to respond by running toward God rather than blaming Him and running away.

THE CURRENCY OF INTIMACY

GOD WAITS FOR YOU TO COMMUNICATE
WITH HIM. YOU HAVE INSTANT,
DIRECT ACCESS TO GOD. GOD LOVES
MANKIND SO MUCH, AND IN A VERY
SPECIAL SENSE HIS CHILDREN, THAT
HE HAS MADE HIMSELF AVAILABLE TO
YOU AT ALL TIMES. — WESLEY L.
DUEWEL

The currency of intimacy is time.

It really is as simple as that. You will never discover or develop a deep and satisfying prayer life so long as you refuse to prioritize actually praying.

Reading about prayer is not praying. Hearing sermons about prayer or listening to teaching on prayer is not praying.

Only one thing is praying.

Praying!

And to truly break through to a life of prayer takes time. There is no way around this fact.

Our flesh has been so used to having its own way it will certainly protest. Our religion-riddled soul will insist that we cannot pray unless we are moved to do so. But the honest truth is that our spirit is ready right now to pray.

Your inner man craves intimacy with the Father.

You have the opportunity to feed that hunger and find more satisfaction than you ever thought possible, or you can put it off until tomorrow again. And again. And again.

My suspicion is that you don't want to do that. You would not be reading this book if that were the case.

So here's where the rubber meets the road.

When in your daily schedule are you going to shut the door on all other activities and give yourself to the work and wonder of praying?

Look to establish a regular time and place for prayer if you can. Be realistic. Don't in your zealous enthusiasm say that you are going to rise at 3am every day and pray for three hours if hitherto you have not prayed for more than 15 minutes. It will not happen. Like any enterprise you build and develop. Be real, but ambitious. If you have never prayed for half an hour, make that your starting goal. That is certainly attainable for anyone with a hunger to grow in prayer. Then, as you flex your prayer muscles, establish an hour consistently carved into your schedule. Make it an absolute priority, and refuse to make excuses. No other exercise or activity this side of heaven is more significant than the secret prayers of God's people rising to His throne. Your refusal to busy yourself with albeit good natural or religious activities in preference to prayer is the greatest service you can possibly offer the Kingdom.

I spent some time with a lovely couple yesterday, and the husband spoke about not having a sacrificial prayer life. But I don't really think of prayer in terms of sacrifice. It was a strange statement to me but when I backtrack I know what he means. You will have to sacrifice other things if you truly want to make prayer a priority. We each have only 24 hours in a day. Time to pray is time you cannot do something else.

But soon the prayer closet will not be considered a place of sacrifice – not even close. It's a place of utmost pleasure. The place where heart reaches heart, deep calls to deep and heaven and earth meet in the greatest mystery known to man.

PRIORITY NOT PRESCRIPTION

TRUE PRAYER IS MEASURED BY
WEIGHT, NOT BY LENGTH. A SINGLE
GROAN BEFORE GOD MAY HAVE MORE
FULLNESS OF PRAYER IN IT THAN A
FINE ORATION OF GREAT LENGTH. — C.
H. SPURGEON

The tendency of the fleshly mind mixed with religion is to lean toward legalism.

With regard to prayer, for example, it would set specific targets that prove the devoted spirituality of a saint. It may be an hour, or two. Maybe even more. In the last chapter I encouraged you to set a specific time and place to pray. The danger is that your flesh would then measure itself by this new ideal. The amount of minutes spent in prayer is not really the point though.

Legalism always wants to prescribe some clear guideline that can be fulfilled so it can tick a box and do its duty.

Relationship does not work like that. Loving Larna, my wife, is not a duty I fulfil. I love her willingly from my heart, even through hard times. Relationship is a glorious ebb and flow of giving and receiving that ultimately cannot be quantified. Nevertheless, opportunity needs to be provided for that ebb and flow to take place.

But the pursuit of personal prayer and secret seeking cannot be boiled down to the number of minutes and hours spent locked away on your knees. Thank God for that!

Consider the story in the gospels about the widow and her mite. Here was a lady so poverty stricken she literally had no more than a penny to offer to God. Surrounded by rich religious men with their impressive wads and fat offerings, one would naturally tend to measure the relative worth of the offerings by men's standards. More is more – right?

Not in the eyes of Jesus. He saw the pompous and prosperous devotees flaunting their abundance, but it was the unnoticed worshipper that caught His attention. This little lady with her seemingly pitiful offering ravished Jesus' heart.

"See that little old lady?" He urged his disciples. "She has given more than all of these other pretenders put together."

She didn't have much, but what she had she gave.

The rich folks could have been equally impressive to the Lord had their hearts been different. He was not looking at the offering; He was looking at the heart behind the offering. The amount given was secondary to the attitude and motive behind the giving.

The point I'm making here has nothing to do with what you placed in the offering bucket this week. It has to do with a far more scarce and precious commodity than money. Time.

Each of us has time that we can give. Some more than others. We may be like the widow and have only a penny's worth of minutes to freely choose to do with as we please. Or we could be time-rich and have the luxury of giving from an abundance of free time.

God is not counting the seconds. He knows what is possible for you.

We may not all have the privilege of endless hours to offer. But we do all share one reality.

We get to prioritize the time that we do have.

PRIORITY NOT PRESCRIPTION

Building a life of prayer is not always about the amount of hours we are spending seeking God. It is not a matter of prescription, spending an allotted amount of hours praying in order to fulfil a quota. It is instead a matter of priority.

The question we all must answer as honestly as we can is this: what am I doing with the time that I do have?

Jesus said that where our treasure is, that's where our heart will follow. Our treasure both reveals our priorities, and feeds into them. We can shift our priority by intentionally moving our treasure in the direction we want our heart to follow.

Your greatest treasure, the one you can only spend and never save, is time. Time equals life. And if your life belongs to the Lord, it will show up in your calendar. It will show up like the little widow woman, unnoticed and unseen by the bustling world around you, but noticed by the King.

In what way are you prioritizing secret time alone with God? Even if all you have is a seemingly insignificant sliver, dedicate it to the Lord and He will multiply the results beyond anything you could imagine.

And if you have an abundance to offer, a time-rich life to share, be generous and thankful. Don't fill your hours with frivolous pursuits. Seek God with all your heart just as desperately and devotedly as the poor widow who gave all she had in pursuit of God's best for her life.

Time spent seeking God is the greatest investment anyone can ever make.

PRAYER IS NOT LEARNED IN A
CLASSROOM BUT IN THE CLOSET. — E.
M. BOUNDS

I spoke in the last chapter about priority.

Do you make time alone with God a priority?

I was challenged many years ago when I considered the reality that many people are moved by necessity in ways that demand rigorous sacrifices. The man or woman who has to commute to work, for example, thinks nothing of rising before the sun in order to prepare for their journey to work. It becomes a priority because it is deemed necessary. No choice is made each day; it is unquestionably something that must happen.

Why is prayer not considered just as important? Why do we consign prayer to our optional list of activities, and have so many other activities on our essential list?

Surely if we really crave the kind of relationship with God that immerses us in His purposes, we will approach the matter of prayer with the same zeal that we approach other strong motivators in our lives. We will move it across from the optional pile to the essential.

Once the question changes from *should* I pray today, to *when should* I pray today, everything will begin to change for you.

By no longer accepting the option not to pray, you are immediately in a powerful position for transformation of your prayer life. You will begin to be much more intentional and actively seek ways to recover the time that you need to really seek your Father's face and hand.

Over the years for me this pursuit has taken many forms. It has meant taking my lunch hours at work and dedicating them to private prayer sitting in my car or hidden on local scrubland behind the offices. It has meant rising early or staying up late to ensure not a day passed without giving God opportunity to speak. It has seen me lock myself in my bedroom and tell myself in no uncertain terms that I will not leave until an hour has passed, or locking myself in the bathroom in homes I have stayed whilst traveling in order to find a private place to pour out my heart.

It has not been a matter of *will I?* But a matter of *where and when will I?* The hunger for Him removes the roadblocks that stand in the way. We have all heard the saying, *where there's a will there's a way.* Nowhere is this more true than in prayer. If your will has yielded to the necessity of prayer, and your soul has tasted the wonders of His good presence, nothing will stop you finding avenues to get alone and entwine your heart with His.

RECOVERING YOUR INHERITANCE

NO DUTY IS MORE EARNESTLY
IMPRESSED UPON US IN SCRIPTURE
THAN THE DUTY OF CONTINUAL
COMMUNION WITH HIM. — DAVID
MCINTYRE

A strong, vibrant and satisfying relationship with God is your inheritance as a child of the Most High. Jesus did not die to forgive our sins so much as He died to introduce us to the Father. His end game was not clearing up the mess we had gotten ourselves into; it was restoring what we lost in the first place!

Another favorite verse...

> "He... brought thee out ...to bring thee in, to give thee their land for an inheritance, as it is this day."
>
> — DEUTERONOMY 4:37–38 KJV

He brought you out, to bring you in.

The bringing in is the key thing. That is why Jesus died and rose.

He wants to bring you into your inheritance. It is a place of abundance not scarcity.

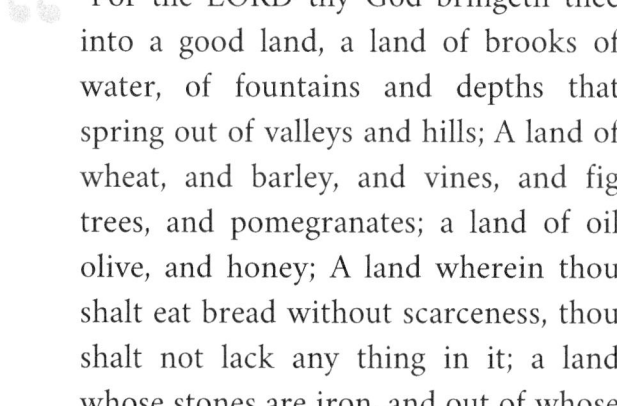 "For the LORD thy God bringeth thee into a good land, a land of brooks of water, of fountains and depths that spring out of valleys and hills; A land of wheat, and barley, and vines, and fig trees, and pomegranates; a land of oil olive, and honey; A land wherein thou shalt eat bread without scarceness, thou shalt not lack any thing in it; a land whose stones are iron, and out of whose hills thou mayest dig brass. When thou hast eaten and art full, then thou shalt bless the LORD thy God for the good land which he hath given thee."

— DEUTERONOMY 8:7–10 KJV

Discovering and developing a secret life of prayer does require discipline, but the habits and sacrifices that you need to make to prioritize private prayer pale in comparison to the benefits you reap when you do so.

Never forget that your Father has more set aside for you to enjoy than you could ever dare to ask or think. His rewards are reserved for you alone to claim. No one else can take what belongs to you. Sadly, however, the majority of Christians do not even realize that they have inheritance waiting to be claimed.

The pathway of prayer that you have embarked upon is one that will bring you into the life God has prepared. He wants to know you, and to be known by you.

Claim your inheritance and take your promised land. Every family in Israel had an allotted portion of the land that belonged to them. When God brought them in they claimed their portion. Caleb had his mountain and never let go! Even at 85 years old he ran after what he knew was his *(Joshua 14:10-11)*.

Be like Caleb and never settle until you sit on your own plot of spiritual ground, enjoying the fruits of your relationship with Jesus.

EVERY GREAT MOVEMENT OF GOD CAN
BE TRACED TO A KNEELING FIGURE. —
DWIGHT L. MOODY

I love the word *cultivate*. There is something so earthy and real about it. It speaks of an investment of time and effort in order to bring forth a desired harvest. It speaks to me of sensitivity and willingness to pour oneself into a process of deepening and developing something so the richness and fruit of it can be savored.

It takes time to cultivate friendships. It takes time to deepen relationship.

The call of this book is for you to cultivate a rich prayer life.

Today's pressured society pushes for instant results. We *say* a few prayers and wonder why our life has not changed. We dedicate the dregs of our time to private seeking - a snatched few minutes here and there outside our over-busy schedule, and wonder why our connection with Heaven lacks something of the life we see in Jesus and other men and women of God in the Bible and beyond.

But the relational side of prayer can be likened more to agriculture than to industry. It is not a matter of pressing the right buttons or pulling the correct levers. In prayer we put down roots into the soil of God's love and faithfulness. We reach up and branch out, bearing spiritual fruit.

> "And the remnant that is escaped of the house of Judah shall yet again take root downward, and bear fruit upward."
>
> — 2 KINGS 19:30 KJV

Cultivation also speaks of the long haul. I was in the woods with my wife and two youngest boys last week, and as we ventured deeper into the forest the trees grew sturdier and taller, until we came across some majestic trees so broad and high that we felt dwarfed by their grandeur.

No one needed to tell us that these beautiful, immovable kings of the forest did not spring up overnight. We knew that they were established over many hundreds of years.

Come to your prayer life knowing that God is not wanting a slot machine relationship with you, one where you pop in a quick coin of prayer every so often in time of need, hoping for an immediate payout. Papa is waiting patiently for you to dig deep layers of intimate conversation and encounter.

From this kind of consistent communion over time a history is built whereby there will be a million milestones that speak to you of His heart and faithfulness, His provision and promises. Instead of staring at a blank page when you consider your connection to the Godhead, you will have an abundance of instances built over time that you can look back upon and that will secure you in any turbulence you might presently be enduring. Your encounters will feed like a gushing river into a future watered by faith in the words you have heard and your catalogue of God's goodness.

One of the paradoxes of prayer is a growing maturity balanced by a growing childlike dependence. As we mature we actually become more childlike in our simplicity and trust.

CHILDLIKE

PRAY, AND LET GOD WORRY. — MARTIN
LUTHER

Too many people come to prayer with such a serious super-spiritual mindset that it cramps their development. We don't come to the closet as spiritual giants; we come as children who serve a giant God. In private prayer, especially in the early stages of learning to pray and extending your prayer vocabulary, a childlike attitude is such a powerful aid to growth.

We grow through play.

Being willing to work with God, laugh at yourself, try new things, explore the realm of prayer with creativity and playfulness, trusting Papa and allowing Him to delight in your efforts, transforms the prayer closet from a claustrophobic enclave to a wide open place to leap and dance through.

Don't get hung up on 'doing it right' - the Holy Spirit will lead you, and if you run off on some tangent He is more than able to tug on your walking-reins and get you back on track.

There is a reckless confidence and curiosity that children display that the Father wants you to enjoy in the realms of prayer.

Be willing to try new things. Open your mind, heart and mouth to unusual utterances and sounds. The Bible in Romans 8 speaks of groans and sighs being part of the vast vocabulary of heartfelt prayer. Tongues of men and angels are made available to the believer to explore and exercise. Proclamations, prophecy, tongues and interpretation, new songs and Spirit inspired expressions - all of these are in the toy box, later to become the toolbox of matured prayer. But don't be afraid or ashamed to begin in the toy box and step out with an immature understanding. So long as we feign maturity it becomes hard for the Holy Spirit to grow us further.

When Jesus spoke of the Spirit, He described His work within as like springs and rivers flowing from our inner man:

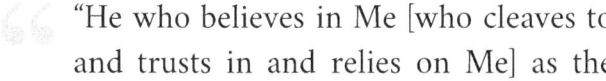 "He who believes in Me [who cleaves to and trusts in and relies on Me] as the

Scripture has said, From his innermost being shall flow [continuously] springs and rivers of living water."

— JOHN 7:38 AMPLIFIED

Elsewhere the work of the Spirit is compared to mysterious effects of the wind:

"The wind blows (breathes) where it wills; and though you hear its sound, yet you neither know where it comes from nor where it is going. So it is with everyone who is born of the Spirit."

— JOHN 3:8 AMPLIFIED

The Holy Spirit is untamed, playful, and spontaneous. The character of the Spirit is not staid and hemmed in by tradition. He is exuberant. Excited. Passionate. Inspirational in the real sense of the word - the very breath of God moving in the earth wherever and however He wills.

Let Him carry you, and learn by faltering experience to move with Him. As you do so, even to your own joyful embarrassment (remember, we are talking about private prayer here so no one else is going to see or judge you), you will slowly build confidence and become familiar with His different moods and movements. It becomes easy to flow with Him, not leaning on your own understanding or knowledge, but instead fully entrusting yourself to His leading. Like a child being led by their parent, He will take you to places you could never reach alone.

Just last week, in my garage that I have claimed as my closet, He had me dancing around with flailing abandonment one day, and the next singing wild songs in other tongues. Then there was the morning where He led me to lie on the floor and just listen, and the day we took the words of God from the book of Ephesians and turned that entire letter - all six chapters - into a personal heartfelt prayer. Alongside these, the tears, the groans, the yearning cries for more. The silent times of relaxed communion, just drinking in His presence and basking in His love. Taken together, it becomes a textured and interesting experience filled with the living substance of prayer. And by that I mean the living substance of His Person. He, the Holy Spirit, is the Spirit of prayer and supplication. When was the last time you invited Him in?

Being open to His leading in this way, with childlike willingness to step out and have fun, frolicking with Him as well as yielding to the deeper more grave expressions of faith, makes for a rich and varied prayer life.

Texture in prayer is so important. A layered, engaging experience of prayer will keep you coming back for more. An insipid boring same-old-same-old approach where you leave no room for making mistakes or having fun in the Presence of God will soon lose any appeal.

Come like a child, and God will raise a hero!

BROADEN YOUR PRAYER & PRAISE VOCABULARY

THE WORD OF GOD IS THE FOOD BY
WHICH PRAYER IS NOURISHED AND
MADE STRONG. — E. M. BOUNDS

When we talk about intimacy, we are talking about heart communion. A mingling of spirits and a clear vision and understanding of one another that goes far below the surface. The bridge to the heart of another person is words. Through words you are able to express and communicate your deepest desires and thoughts that otherwise would remain a mystery to others. Through words we can enter the heart and imagination of another and bring them into our world. Their own secret garden is opened to us as they express themselves and we begin to see as they see.

God chose words as His primary avenue to express His heart. Jesus was the Word made flesh. The heart of God expressed through the Bible clothed Himself with humanity and walked among us. Jesus and the Word are one.

Through the Bible we enter into the mind and heart of Almighty God. He seeds our imagination with Heavenly reality.

Like prayer, satan wants to smear the bible with the designation, "boring, dry and lifeless." He wants to so suck the life and joy from your times of communion with God in His Word that you feel there's nothing there but shallow marks on a thin page. But God's Words are so much more than that. They are doorways to His world.

Jesus said that His words are "spirit and life" (John 6:63). How powerful to realize that spirit speaks to spirit through the words of Scripture.

One of the ways that I have engaged more deeply with Scripture is to approach it as if I am learning a new language. It is the language of heavenly realms, and, as with any culture, becoming fluent opens the entire culture of that society or country to you. We may begin with just a few phrases. "Hello" "What is your name?" "Do you speak English?" At this stage the level of fellowship is limited and somewhat superficial. But as we develop our vocabulary the communion and companionship we experience within that new culture expands in tandem with our growing ability to hear, speak and understand the language, and therefore express our heart more clearly and grasp what others are wanting to say to us.

So it is with the Scriptures. In an increasingly Biblically illiterate society, it behoves us as followers of Christ to ensure fluency in God's ways and words.

With regard to prayer this is essential. A rich deposit of God's Word and an understanding of His ways increases our effectiveness, and also the depths to which we can dive in private devotion.

I will share just two ways that have helped me in my quest for more of God in this regard, both very simple and easy to apply.

First was a combing of the New Testament for every instance where God speaks of who I am in Christ. Throughout the New Testament, particularly the epistles, there are hundreds of places where we find the words, "in him" "in Christ" "in whom" and other revelations of who we have now become through the blood of Jesus and our union with Him. I underlined and wrote every one of them down. Spoke them out. Claimed them, believed them, and appropriated them in my life.

Another, and this is one of my favorites, is to walk slowly through the rich forest of the Psalms and underline any words or phrases that I can add to my praise vocabulary. Pick the fruits from the trees, smell the flowers lining the pathways, breathe in the fresh gusts and breezes of divinity as they blow through the branches. This book above all others is a garden to be savored. The book of Psalms is such a raw expressive explosion of humanity encountering the heavenly and is replete with many wonderful ways to expand our prayer and praise vocabulary thus enhancing our own times of private devotion with Papa, Son and Holy Ghost.

And, as always, the learning is fully cooked only when it is applied. To truly grasp and become fluent in a language generally requires immersion in the culture of the people you want to communicate with. There is nothing more effective to increase our fluency than being in and spending significant time in the very culture we want to enter, speaking their language, eating their food, and living in their community.

So it is here with prayer. The Godhead is a community of love you have been invited to join. Write down the expressions you discover in the Word and when you come into your secret place, rehearse them. Don't do this dispassionately - put your heart into it just as the original writers and singers would have. Make the words of Scripture your own and they will become the catalyst for your own unique expressions of adoration, frustration or praise to the Father. Be real and honest, and don't hold anything back.

As you do you will experience a whole new level of fellowship opening before you. The Living Word will speak through the written Word, and when you hear Him everything changes!

DIALOGUE WITH GOD

PRAYER IS NOT MONOLOGUE, BUT
DIALOGUE; GOD'S VOICE IS ITS MOST
ESSENTIAL PART. LISTENING TO GOD'S
VOICE IS THE SECRET OF THE
ASSURANCE THAT HE WILL LISTEN TO
MINE. — ANDREW MURRAY

P rayer is not meant to be a monologue, where we throw a multitude of words heavenward, say amen and leave the room.

God wants to speak to us on all occasions, and has made provision for us to be able to hear him in lots of different ways.

This richness of dynamic dialogue with God is what makes prayer so exciting. Throughout the Bible we read of men and women who entered into a conversational intimacy with the Father, and that same privilege is open to us.

God speaks in many ways including but not limited

to dreams and visions, through the written or spoken Word, or in the still small voice on the inside of your heart. It could be an audible voice, although I think that is rare. More often God will speak in ways that require us to listen carefully and intentionally. He is interested in relationship and relationships are developed most strongly when we grow ever more sensitive to one another's voice and communication.

Hearing God is a whole other book, but as I said earlier, we learn to pray by praying. It may sound simplistic, but we learn to hear by listening.

I love the words that the Holy Spirit inspired in this regard:

> "Incline your ear…"
>
> — PROVERBS 4:20 NKJV

Lean in to listen.

Still the other noise of life that hounds for your attention and crave his whispers.

When you do this you will surely begin to sense what He is saying to you. Clarity comes as we hone our ear to perceive what God is speaking, and then don't discount what we hear.

A big problem I have noticed with people is that they do hear Him, but immediately brush off what they hear as their own thoughts. They see a picture and ascribe it to the pizza they ate the night before.

Of course, we do get it wrong sometimes, or we misunderstand or misinterpret, but that should not be our default position or expectancy. As children of God it is natural for us to receive from Him. Our eyes and ears have been opened to perceive the spiritual world, and especially His voice.

 "My sheep hear my voice…"

— JOHN 10:27 KJV

This is the place we begin. By faith.

"I am His sheep. I hear His voice!"

That should be your absolute expectation. Know also that hearing God, and interpreting what you hear with clarity, is something that you can develop and improve at. How do we improve? We do it! We practice it.

Begin by asking questions.

"What do you have to say to me today, Lord?"

"How do you see me, Lord?"

"What would you like to say to this person to encourage them?"

Start with simple questions and listen for the answer. Yes/No questions are always worth practicing with. As you grow in confidence the dialogue expands and the conversation deepens.

Don't ever settle for one way traffic in prayer. Real excitement and adventure arise from conversing with Heaven and seeing His words go to work in your life.

Just as Jesus described His mode of operation as not doing or saying anything that He had not already seen or heard His Father doing, so it can be for you and I.

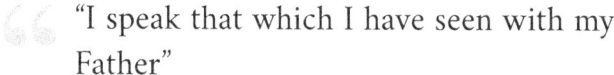 "I speak that which I have seen with my Father"

— JOHN 8:38 KJV

One of my favorite ways to dialogue, and to be brutally honest one I avoided for years (to my own regret) is through what some call two-way journaling. This concept of journaling is so much more than keeping a spiritual diary. It is a means of ongoing conversation.

Mark Virkler's book, *4 Keys To Hearing God's Voice*, impacted my life significantly in this regard. (https://www.cwgministries.org/Four-Keys-to-Hearing-Gods-Voice)

Essentially the four keys he encourages everyone to practice are very simple:

1. **Still your heart and mind** before God.
2. **Look for vision**, looking to Jesus, letting God use the faculty of your imagination to show you pictures.
3. **Listen for spontaneous thoughts** bubbling up from your spirit - be open to God interjecting and don't dismiss what you hear.
4. **Journal your conversations** - write down your thoughts, prayers and questions, but don't stop there. Scribe God's responses. When I began doing this, first writing down my question, and then by faith writing His answer, freely and spontaneously not second-guessing myself, I was literally swept away at what began to happen. Among other things, God spoke to me about the exact time I would move home, specific words for

friends and family, incredible insights about my own soul and my calling to write, and so much more. He navigated me through some of the toughest most insecure times I have ever experienced, using journaling to steer my course. Today we talk and journal together about everything. On a practical level, I use an app on my iPad called Penzu for my journaling, but pencil and paper work just as well.

Whatever way you choose to work your walk, don't settle for less than God's best. A dry, spiritless prayer life is so far removed from God's ideal for you that you should literally rebuke even the thought that it would be that way for you.

One more thing with regard to listening. Stop trying so hard! A sure fire intimacy killer in spiritual things is the fire and fury of our own fleshly efforts to produce spiritual results.

Rest is the atmosphere and environment in which His voice is most clearly heard. Not necessarily natural rest, but a serenity of spirit that has ceased striving to please God or *make* things happen, and instead by faith has accepted His abundant provision.

Hebrews 4 is by far one of my favorite chapters in all of Scripture.

 "There remaineth therefore a rest to the people of God. For he that is entered into his rest, he also hath ceased from his own works, as God did from his.

Let us labor therefore to enter into that rest, lest any man fall after the same example of unbelief."

— HEBREWS 4:9–11 KJV

The context of this is found in verse 4, "Today, if you will hear his voice…"

Papa wants to speak to you today!

Are you listening?

Have you closed the door on other things to give Him opportunity?

WANT TO START JOURNALLING?

Begin the process of 2-way journalling with the **My Secret Place Prayer Journal** - over 200 inspirational pages waiting for your conversations with Papa.

You can also check out our range of journals and spiritual notebooks here...

PureRead Prayer Journals and Notebooks

PRACTICAL KEYS TO DISCOVERING AND DEVELOPING A SECRET LIFE OF PRAYER

PRAYER DOES NOT FIT US FOR THE GREATER WORK; PRAYER IS THE GREATER WORK. — OSWALD CHAMBERS

As we draw to a close let's ask ourselves what we plan to actually do with this passionate desire that we carry in our spirit. Revelation is certainly beautiful, but application is what will shape your destiny.

Forgive me if I repeat myself in this chapter, but do bear with me as we remember some key points.

What are you doing to prioritize time alone with God in unnoticed, private, secret prayer and worship? Not serving God in activities, or public gatherings, but building your hidden relationship with the Lord?

If we truly love Him we will look for ways to make

this happen. The deepest most intimate moments – the times when we know another person more intimately than any other time – are not the times on public display.

It is the same with our walk with God. If we genuinely desire true intimacy and closeness with God. If we want to reveal ourselves to Him and have Him open Himself to us in deeper more satisfying ways, it will happen in private.

Building this secret life is not easy sometimes. We are so used to activity, and so inclined to seek our satisfaction from other sources. But the rewards of a life spent discovering and developing a secret life of worship and prayer far outweigh any other reward we might receive from people.

Ask yourself in what ways you can cultivate a rich and fulfilling secret life of prayer.

Here are some of the things that I have found helpful to practically do that:

1. CREATE AN ENVIRONMENT FOR WORSHIP AND PRAYER.

Have a specific place that you set aside for secret prayer. Somewhere that becomes associated with intimacy and seeking Heaven for you. I have had lots of these places over the years, everything from a favorite armchair at 4am in the morning to an empty warehouse at the close of the day. My own places of personal daily retreat have included a piece of scrubland behind the offices of the newspaper I worked for (during my lunch hour), the passenger side seat of my car, pushed back so I could kneel in front of it with my face in the seat so other people in the workplace car park could not see me as I prayed (again, during lunch breaks when the weather was not good for scrubland prayer), a tiny ramshackle shed in my back garden in the small seaside town we were pastoring in (that got so hot in the summer I thought I would faint!), the bottom of a stairwell in the church I worked at, an empty warehouse where 4 or 5 of us would gather from 6am to 8am every day before heading to work. Presently my prayer closet is a garage on the property we rent. Love will always find a way and a place to meet its beloved. Having a specific personal place that you begin to associate with prayer and worship soon trains your body, soul and spirit to enter in quickly and seamlessly, rather than fighting distractions all the time. It is not essential, but can be very helpful.

2. PRIORITIZE TIME AND CREATE A HABIT

I have found that if I leave my prayer life to chance, seeking God just when I feel moved or prompted to pray, it simply does not happen, or it is so sporadic that it's virtually pointless because no real place of authority in the spirit is built. God promised manna, bread from heaven, every day. If the Israelites failed to gather and consume it that day, it was gone the following morning. It's the same for us in private devotion. God wants to speak, but if we don't turn to hear, that day's special is taken off the menu forever. A life too busy for God is a life too busy! We miss out on so much that could sustain and nourish us if only we would make fellowship with God our number one pursuit.

3. LEARN THE SKILL OF SECRET PRAYER

We learn a skill by doing something again and again. In the early stages every skill worth learning has its fair share of frustrations and failures. When the rubber meets the road, we grow and develop not by reading about something, not by hearing someone talk about it, not by watching a series on TV about it. We learn to pray by DOING prayer. We learn to pray by praying. We learn to worship by worshipping. Our flesh nature is like an unbroken horse, reluctant to be tamed. The only way to break the strength of an unyielded nature is to force it to wait on God. Lock the door and don't let yourself off the hook. Soon enough your spirit will take the place of ascendency over your flesh and begin to press in. One of my teachers put it this way – we move from DESIRE to DISCIPLINE to DELIGHT. Once we have tasted the fruit of secret relationship with Papa, nothing else can ever satisfy!

Remember this –

We don't HAVE to worship – we GET to worship!

We don't HAVE to pray – We GET to pray!

WE don't HAVE to read the Bible – we GET to read the Bible!

The proximity we have been offered is a privilege, not a burden or a requirement. How amazing it is that we CAN know God intimately! Why would anyone in their right mind pass over such an amazing open door?

4. BROADEN YOUR VOCABULARY

There is a great deal more richness to worship than "Hallelujah, praise the Lord, Hallelujah, praise the Lord" ad infinitum. The Bible is a dictionary of praise, and teaches us the vocabulary of the spirit. Study is not supposed to be dry and lifeless; it feeds our spirit with an abundance that then becomes fruit on our lips. The Psalms of course are a perfect example of imperfect people worshipping God from the depth of their hearts. We can do the same, but we need to broaden our stock of expressions and our understanding of who God is to really experience the wealth that awaits us. Make the Bible your close companion, knowing that its words are not natural words; they are "spirit and life" (John 6:63).

5. BE A CHILD

God is not looking for neat, perfect praise. In secret we don't have to play any role, or pretend to be mature, or have it all together – we can just be our imperfect, silly or serious self without worrying about what anyone else says, sees or thinks. Papa is delighted when His children come to Him freely and openly, enjoying Him and letting go of their hang ups. There is a place for serious intercession, but it must be balanced with light hearted friendship and joyful expressions of worship too. I guess the point is that we need to learn the art of avoiding the temptation to try and be someone or something in God's presence, and just straight up be ourselves, warts and all. Pour out your praise before Him, and also your poison. Hold nothing back. God is not nervous or offended or surprised by anything you bring to Him, and the more vulnerable and real you can be the better. Openness and freedom in the secret place gives Papa access to the woundedness as well as the wonder. Recognize that He loves and enjoys us just as we are, wherever we are on this incredible journey to intimacy with Him.

CONSISTENCY VS FERVENCY

THE VALUE OF CONSISTENT PRAYER IS
NOT THAT HE WILL HEAR US, BUT THAT
WE WILL HEAR HIM. ~WILLIAM MCGILL

As you know, I am an advocate of intimacy, and the first to champion fervency. I am also very aware, however, that zeal alone does not guarantee a rich and lasting prayer life. In fact, if heat and steam are what you seek the many days of simmering and seeking that will will be required of you may well lead to despondency. Over the years, I have discovered that a life of pray is one that ebbs and flows. Each season will bring it's own blessings and challenges and we must never limit the Lord as to how He wants to work.

Remaining consistent through the unremarkable seasons seems to be the price a praying man or woman pays for those ordained times of encounter that come from the sovereign hand of the Father. One without the other is rare. Yes, we can storm-chase the anointing running from meeting to meeting, but that is not the way to put down roots. Roots are grown in the dark unseen places of private prayer and devotion far more than they are in public forums. Those seemingly lonely hours spent alone reaching for Heaven's touch are never wasted.

It can be likened to building a house. Passion for the project plays it's part, but is the laying of one brick upon another that leads to the establishment of a dwelling. So it is in the spirit. Every moment, minute, hour and day we give over to obedient seeking lays one more brick. What seems so laborious and unremarkable at the outset, gradually begins to take form. Instead of just trying to pray, you will feel yourself step-by-step entering into a life of prayer. You are building a dwelling place for God to inhabit in your life. The trying hours of spiritual sweat that lay the foundations and put down each individual brick becomes a place of abiding. In the same way that you step across the threshhold of your natural house and immediately feel at 'home', so it will be in the spirit. The place of prayer will become your place of abiding.

And the best thing about this? Well, to be honest there are many benefits, but here's just a few…

Prayer becomes your place of escape from the fury of life and the problems you face. Instead of hiding in other sometimes negative behaviors, you now have somewhere to run that offer's solutions. Scripture tells us that God's name is like a strong tower into which we can run and find safe haven (Proverbs 18:10).

Prayer becomes that place you can be yourself more than any other. Just as your natural home is where the mask is peeled away, so the house of prayer becomes one into which you confidently step without any pressure to perform.

Prayer is your place of refreshment. It is the one place you run to for affirmation from the only One who really matters, rather than earnestly seeking it in places that leave you empty.

You and Papa are partners in the building of this glorious dwelling, and as you work together over the days, weeks, years and decades, the abode of prayerfulness that you have entered into will expand beyond your wildest expectations. You will discover incredible treasures hidden in it's many rooms. Sometimes Papa will usher you into entire wings of the building that you never knew existed.

I hope this picture of building a dwelling place for God's presence is making sense. I personally feel such excitement and anticipation as I write about it. The very idea of your wide eyed delight as Papa opens the doors to you makes me want to jump up and shout with joy!

And the pathway is not complicated. It is not reserved for some navy seal of spirituality. The very fact that it is apparently unimpressive and incredibly ordinary is all the more glorious. Like the wardrobe that led to Narnia in C.S. Lewis' classic children's story, *The Lion, the Witch and the Wardrobe*, one would never have known from the outside that something so everyday could be the doorway to entire realms yet unexplored.

It is so simple, and can be summed up in one boring word.

Consistency.

Daily coming into God's presence. Understanding that swinging the axe one more time is what will bring the tree to the ground. Laying just one more brick to develop the dwelling. Taken in isolation, twenty minutes here or ten minutes there appears so insignificant. But a prayer life is not built in an instant. It is not an event. It is a lifestyle of sensitive obedience to the promptings of the Spirit lived out in the everyday challenges that leads a man or woman to the place where they can truly say that they know God.

Never underestimate the power of your choice to pray today. However uninspired or disappointing it may sometimes feel, it is one more step toward your next life-changing encounter with the Godhead.

Way too many people give up because they have been falsely taught that prayer should be one big heavenly party. Instead it more like a marriage. Many honest ordinary days make up the rich layered nature of intimate relationship, and years of walking side by side fuse two hearts into one. Yes, of course there are intense times of intimacy. Absolutely there are explosive engagements that forge the relationship in unusual ways unique to the partners, but such encounters are not the flavor of every day. Finding and deeply appreciating the value of your love in the seemingly mundane disciplines of daily routine is mighty powerful. So it is in our daily walk with God.

Fervency is a deep river. On the surface there may be the froth and billowing of feeling, and this is sometimes what people refer to as fervency; the overt emotion present in passionate prayer. But feeling is not the driving force, just the outward show of something deeper. My daughter is an elite gymnast, competing for her country in Rhythmic Gymnastics. It is not feeling that keeps her in the gym for several hours every day, it is fervency. She does not always 'feel' like training, but her desire to reach her goals drives her there every day. Her fervency is not proven by overwhelming feeling, it is proven by faithfulness.

If your prayer life is determined by the fickle waves of feeling it will be inconsistent and real progress will elude you. Believe me, if I prayed only when I 'feel' like it, my times of prayer would be the pepper of life rather than the meat on the plate. A day here, a day there. A house is not built with hit-or-miss bricks placed wherever they happen to land. It is built course-upon-course, row-upon-row. Build your prayer life in the same way and soon you have a place of abiding that makes prayer a wholly different experience.

Build a dwelling place for God's presence. Lean into prayer with the same intent you lean into other things you want to learn and develop in your life. No other skill or practice is more important or satisfying. Overcome the resistance of your flesh inwardly, and the pressure of the devil outwardly. That means praying when you do not feel like praying. Priotitize prayer. Instead of fitting prayer around the responsibilities and demands of everyday life, fit your everyday responsibilities and demands around your determination to pray each day. I promise that you will not be disappointed!

WHEN THE DEVIL SEES A MAN OR
WOMAN WHO REALLY BELIEVES IN
PRAYER, WHO KNOWS HOW TO PRAY,
AND WHO REALLY DOES PRAY, AND,
ABOVE ALL, WHEN HE SEES A WHOLE
CHURCH ON ITS FACE BEFORE GOD IN
PRAYER, HE TREMBLES AS MUCH AS HE
EVER DID, FOR HE KNOWS THAT HIS
DAY IN THAT CHURCH OR COMMUNITY
IS AT AN END. — R.A. TORREY

J esus said something very interesting. It is
recorded in the book of John:

"I sent you to reap that whereon ye
bestowed no labour: **other men
laboured, and ye are entered into their
labours**."

— JOHN 4:38 KJV

Sometimes we forget that prayer is timeless. Prayers that the patriarchs prayed and prophesied came to pass thousands of years later in the person of Jesus. It is good to remember this when we are praying, that although we may not see immediate answers, our efforts in the spirit are not without merit. Our Father has heard, and answered!

I find this through incredibly encouraging when I read of men and women of old who prayed; they prayed BIG prayers, nation-changing intercessions. They labored in the spirit, in the ways that Paul speaks of in a number of places in his letters:

> "Epaphras, who is *one* of you, a servant of Christ, saluteth you, **always labouring fervently for you in prayers**, that ye may stand perfect and complete in all the will of God."
>
> — COLOSSIANS 4:12 KJV

> "My little children, of whom **I travail in birth again until Christ be formed in you**"
>
> — GALATIANS 4:19 KJV

There is a spiritual labor that has taken place, one into which we are entering. We are not starting from zero. Symbolically, the prayer bowls in heaven are filled and ready to pour. Great men and women of fervent faith have poured their lives out before the throne, and we in our generation could be the recipient of all the blessings they obtained. We too should be pouring our own selves into this great work, knowing that generations to come will benefit from the overflow of our fire filled praying.

I can almost see the great cloud of witnesses spoken of in Hebrews 12:1 leaning over the balcony of Heaven, cheering as they see the long awaited answers to their most cherished petitions coming to fruition in our generation.

I draw tremendous strength and inspiration, therefore, from quotes by such saints that have been gathered over the decades.

I have shared a handful at the opening of each chapter of this book, and many of the journals we have designed and sell are also packed with them (check out our current range here http://pureread.com/christian-prayer-journals-and-notebooks/).

I want to share some of my favorites with you here,

to throw fuel on the fire of your intention. Pray, my dear friends, and never give up…

> "Our praying needs to be pressed and pursued with an energy that never tires, a persistency which will not be denied, and a courage which never fails." — E. M. Bounds

> "God does nothing but by prayer, and everything with it." — John Wesley

> "Prayer does not fit us for the greater work; prayer is the greater work." — Oswald Chambers

> "In no other way can the believer become as fully involved with God's work especially the work of world evangelism as in intercessory prayer… When the prayer warrior intercedes, he forgets his personal need and focuses all of his faith and prayer attention on others. To intercede is to mediate. It is to stand between a lost being and an Almighty God, praying that this person will come to know about God and His

salvation." — Dick Eastman, *The Hour That Changes The World*

"Search for a person who claims to have found Christ apart from someone else's prayer, and your search may go on forever." — E. Bauman

"Have you any days of fasting and prayer? Storm the throne of grace and persevere therein, and mercy will come down." — John Wesley

"No one's a firmer believer in the power of prayer than the devil; not that he practices it, but he suffers from it." — Guy H. King

"Perhaps you will have to spend hours on your knees or upon your face before the throne. Never mind. Wait. God will do great things for you if you will wait for Him. Yield to Him. Cooperate with Him." — John Smith

"If the church would only awaken to her responsibility of intercession, we could well evangelize the world in a short time. It is not God's plan that the world be merely evangelized ultimately. It should be evangelized in every generation. There should be a constant gospel witness in every corner of the world so that no sinner need close his eyes in death without hearing the gospel, the good news of salvation through Christ." — T. S. Hegre

"O brother, pray; in spite of Satan, pray; spend hours in prayer; rather neglect friends than not pray; rather fast, and lose breakfast, dinner, tea, and supper— and sleep too—than not pray. And we must not talk about prayer, we must pray in right earnest. The Lord is near. He comes softly while the virgin slumbers." — Andrew A. Bonar

"Next to the wonder of seeing my Savior will be, I think, the wonder that I made so little use of the power of prayer." — D. L. Moody

"A day without prayer is a day without blessing, and a life without prayer is a life without power." — Edwin Harvey

"To strive in prayer means to struggle through those hindrances which would restrain or even prevent us entirely from continuing in persevering prayer. It means to be so watchful at all times that we can notice when we become slothful in prayer and that we go to the Spirit of prayer to have this remedied. In this struggle, too, the decisive factor is the Spirit of prayer." — O. Hallesby

"Quit playing, start praying. Quit feasting, start fasting. Talk less with men, talk more with God. Listen less to men, listen to the words of God. Skip travel, start travail." — Leonard Ravenhill

"It is a tremendously hard thing to pray aright, yea, it is verily the science of all sciences." — Martin Luther

"The main lesson about prayer is just this: Do it! Do it! **DO IT!** You want to be *taught* to pray. My answer is: *pray and never* faint, and then you shall never fail." — John Laidlaw

"Prayer—secret, fervent, believing prayer—lies at the root of all personal godliness." — Carey's Brotherhood, Serampore

"None can believe how powerful prayer is, and what it is able to effect, but those who have learned it by experience. It is a great matter when in extreme need to take hold on prayer. I know, whenever I have prayed earnestly, that I have been amply heard, and have obtained more than I prayed for. God indeed sometimes delayed, but at last He came." — Martin Luther

"You know the value of prayer: it is precious beyond all price. Never, never neglect it." — Sir Thomas Buxton

"Prayer is the first thing, the second thing, the third thing necessary to a minister. Pray, then my dear brother; pray, pray, pray." — Edward Payson

"It is not enough to begin to pray, nor to pray aright; nor is it enough to continue for a time to pray; but we must patiently, believingly, continue in prayer until we obtain an answer; and further we have not only to continue in prayer unto the end, but we have also to believe that God does hear us, and will answer our prayers. Most frequently we fail in not continuing in prayer until the blessing is obtained, and in not expecting the blessing." — George Müller

"Each time, before you intercede, be quiet first, and worship God in His glory. Think of what He can do, and how He delights to hear the prayers of His redeemed people. Think of your place and privilege in Christ, and expect great things!" — Andrew Murray

"The reason why we obtain no more in prayer is because we expect no more. God usually answers us according to our own hearts." — Richard Alleine

"Satan cannot deny but that great wonders have been wrought by prayer. As the spirit of prayer goes up, so his kingdom goes down. Satan's stratagems against prayer are three. First, if he can, he will keep thee from prayer. If that be not feasible, secondly, he will strive to interrupt thee in prayer. And, thirdly, if that plot takes not, he will labour to hinder the success of thy prayer." — William Gurnall

"The devil is aware that one hour of close fellowship, hearty converse with God in prayer, is able to pull down what he hath been contriving and building many a year." — Flavel

"Beware in your prayers, above everything else, of limiting God, not only by unbelief, but by fancying that you know what He can do. Expect unexpected things 'above all that we ask or think.'" — Andrew Murray

"The devil is not put to flight by a courteous request. He meets us at every turn, contends for every inch, and our progress has to be registered in heart's blood and tears." — Charles E. Cowman

"To the man who prays habitually (not only when he feels like it—that is one of the snares of religion—but also when he does not feel like it) Christ is sure to make Himself real." — James Stewart

"If we would pray aright, the first thing we should do is to see to it that we really get an audience with God, that we really get into His very presence. Before a word of petition is offered, we should have the definite consciousness that we are talking to God, and should believe that He is listening and is going to grant the thing that we ask of Him." — Dr. R. A. Torrey

"Pray for 'all men.' We usually pray more for *things* than we do for *men*. Our prayers should be thrown across their pathway as they rush in their downward course to a lost eternity." — E. M. Bounds

"There are two ways of praying. One asks and hopes; the other craves and waits until he has obtained. It is just this 'until' that characterises the latter. One seeks God and finds Him; the other strives with God and triumphs. The first observes scruiously his daily devotions; the second stays on his knees hours a day, through the night. The first fits in with the ordinary course of life; the second watches, fasts, cries, weeps, sweats blood. The first we have known since we learned to know the Lord; the second…'Lord, teach us to pray.'" — M. Monod

"Prayer is reaching out and after the unseen; fasting, letting go of all that is seen and temporal. Fasting helps express, deepens, confirms the resolution that we are ready to sacrifice anything, even ourselves, to attain what we seek for the kingdom of God." — Andrew Murray

"Great grief prays with great earnestness. Prayer is not a collection of balanced phrases; it is the pouring out of the soul. What is love if it be not fiery? What are prayers if the heart be not ablaze? They are the battles of the soul. In them men wrestle with principalities and powers... The prayer that prevails is not the work of lips and fingertips. It is the cry of a broken heart and the travail of a stricken soul." — Samuel Chadwick

"Effective prayer is prayer that attains what it seeks. It is prayer that moves God, effecting its end." — Charles G. Finney

"Satan's tactics seem to be as follows: He will first of all oppose our breaking through to the place of a real living faith, by all means in his power. He detests the prayer of faith, for it is an authoritative 'notice to quit.' We often have to strive and wrestle in prayer before we attain this quiet, restful faith. And until we break right through and *join hands with God* we have not attained to a real faith at all. However, once we attain to a real faith, all the forces of hell are impotent to annul it. The real battle begins when the prayer of faith has been offered." — J. O. Fraser

"Mind how you pray. Make real business of it. Let it never be a dead formality...plead the promise in a truthful, business-like way...Ask for what you want, because the Lord has promised it. Believe that you have the blessing, and go forth to your work in full assurance of it. Go from your knees singing, because the promise is fulfilled: thus will your prayer be answered...the strength [not length] of your prayer...wins...God; and the strength of prayer lies in your faith in the promise which you pleaded before the Lord." — C. H. Spurgeon

"Where there is much prayer, there will be much of the Spirit; where there is much of the Spirit, there will be ever-increasing prayer." — Andrew Murray

"A godly man is a praying man. As soon as grace is poured in, prayer is poured out. Prayer is the soul's traffic with Heaven; God comes down to us by His Spirit, and we go up to Him by prayer." — T. Watson

"A Christian can obtain deep feeling, by thinking on the object. God is not going to pour these things on you, without any effort on your own. You must cherish the slightest impressions. Take the Bible, and go over the passages that show the condition and prospects of the world. Look at the world, look at your children, and your neighbors and see their condition while they remain in sin; and persevere in prayer and effort till you obtain the blessing of the Spirit of God to dwell in you." — Charles G. Finney

"There is no power like that of prevailing prayer—of Abraham pleading for Sodom, Jacob wrestling in the stillness of the night, Moses standing in the breach, Hannah intoxicated with sorrow, David heart-broken with remorse and grief, Jesus in sweat and blood. Add to this list from the records of the church your personal observation and experience, and always there is cost of passion unto blood. Such prayer prevails. It turns ordinary mortals into men of power. It brings power. It brings fire. It brings rain. It brings life. It brings God." —Samuel Chadwick

"But have we Holy Ghost power—power that restricts the devil's power, pulls down stronghold and obtains promises? Daring delinquents will be damned if they are not delivered from the devil's dominion. What has hell to fear other than a God-anointed, prayer-powered church?" — Leonard Ravenhill

"Every great movement of God can be traced to a kneeling figure." — D. L. Moody

"There is no way that Christians, in a private capacity, can do so much to promote the work of God and advance the kingdom of Christ as by prayer." — Jonathan Edwards

"As it is the business of tailors to make clothes, and the business of cobblers to mend shoes, so it is the business of Christians to pray!" — Martin Luther

"In prayer, it is better to have heart without words, than words without heart. Prayer will make a man cease from sin, or sin entice a man to cease from prayer. The spirit of prayer is more precious than treasures of gold and silver. Pray often, for prayer is a shield to the soul, a sacrifice to God, and a scourge for Satan." — John Bunyan

"You can do more than pray, after you have prayed, but you can never do more than pray until you have prayed." — A. J. Gordon

"Prayer is not overcoming God's reluctance, but laying hold of His willingness." — Martin Luther

"Intercessory prayer is exceedingly prevalent. What wonders it has wrought! The Word of God teems with its marvelous deeds. Believer, thou hast a mighty engine in thy hand, use it well, use it constantly, use it with faith, and thou shalt surely be a benefactor to thy brethren." — C. H. Spurgeon

"More things are wrought by prayer than this world dreams of." — Lord Alfred Tennyson

"Prayer is not a convenient device for imposing our will upon God, or bending his will to ours, but the prescribed way of subordinating our will to his." — John R. W. Stott

"The one concern of the devil is to keep Christians from praying. He fears nothing from prayerless studies, prayerless work, and prayerless religion. He laughs at our toil, mocks at our wisdom, but trembles when we pray." — Samuel Chadwick

"Rich is the person who has a praying friend." — Janice Hughes

"Give me one hundred preachers who fear nothing but sin, and desire nothing but God, and I care not a straw whether they be clergymen or laymen; such alone will shake the gates of hell and set up the kingdom of heaven on earth...God does nothing but in answer to prayer." — John Wesley

"Men are God's method. The church is looking for better methods; God is looking for better men. What the church needs today is not more machinery or better, not new organizations or more and novel methods, but men who the Holy Spirit can use—men of prayer, men mighty in prayer. The Holy Spirit does not come on machinery but on men. He does not anoint plans, but men—men of prayer." — E. M. Bounds

"Our prayers may be awkward. Our attempts may be feeble. But since the power of prayer is in the one who hears it and not in the one who says it, our prayers do make a difference." - Max Lucado

"She (my mother) became a warrior far superior to any epic hero. She became a giant on her knees. With a sword in one hand she battled the enemies of death and disease, and with her other hand stretched toward heaven she kept beseeching God's help and His mercy." - Bishop T.D. Jakes

"There are parts of our calling, works of the Holy Spirit, and defeats of the darkness that will come no other way than through furious, fervent, faith-filled, unceasing prayer." - Beth Moore

"The reality is, my prayers don't change God. But, I am convinced prayer changes me. Praying boldly boots me out of that stale place of religious habit into authentic connection with God Himself." - Lysa TerKeurst

"Is prayer your steering wheel or your spare tire?" - Corrie ten Boom

"To be a Christian without prayer is no more possible than to be alive without breathing." - Martin Luther

"Prayer is simply talking to God like a friend and should be the easiest thing we do each day." - Joyce Meyer

"I have been driven many times upon my knees by the overwhelming conviction that I had no where else to go. My own wisdom and that of all about me seemed insufficient for that day." - Abraham Lincoln

"The prayer offered to God in the morning during your quiet time is the key that unlocks the door of the day. Any athlete knows that it is the start that ensures a good finish." - Adrian Rogers

"God shapes the world by prayer. The more praying there is in the world the better the world will be, the mightier the forces against evil." - Mother Teresa

"To get nations back on their feet, we must first get down on our knees." - Billy Graham

"Prayer should not be regarded as a duty which must be performed, but rather as a privilege to be enjoyed, a rare delight that is always revealing some new beauty." - E.M. Bounds

THE BEGINNING OF GREAT ADVENTURE

MEN MAY SPURN OUR APPEALS, REJECT OUR MESSAGE, OPPOSE OUR ARGUMENTS, DESPISE OUR PERSONS, BUT THEY ARE HELPLESS AGAINST OUR PRAYERS. — J. SIDLOW BAXTER

D*iscovering and Developing a Secret Life of Prayer* is a subject that could be compared to a deep ocean. I feel that I have waded beyond the shallows, but compared to the depths and possibilities that remain to be explored I have just splashed the surface. This prayer thing is an adventure more compelling and exciting than anything else you could ever venture upon.

There is so much more for you! So much the Father wants to bring you into.

The Lord spoke to me last week and told me that He has anointed me to "provoke people to pursuit and purity".

I wasn't sure I liked that word 'provoke' until I looked it up in the dictionary. Positively it means to stimulate or give rise to a reaction or strong emotion in someone, inspire someone to do or feel something, to rouse, give rise to, call or draw forth, bring on, contribute to, stir, move, motivate, fire up or impel someone to action.

If I can do even one of those in your heart as a result of what you have just read, and move you deeper toward that hidden life of satisfaction in God, I will have fulfilled my mandate.

From the burning heart of a fellow traveler and lover of God, I urge you to continue on your own unique and God-soaked journey.

Your next step? Close the door and open your heart and mouth in prayer to Papa. He is ready and waiting.

JOIN THE PRAYER PRINCIPLES
NEWSLETTER...

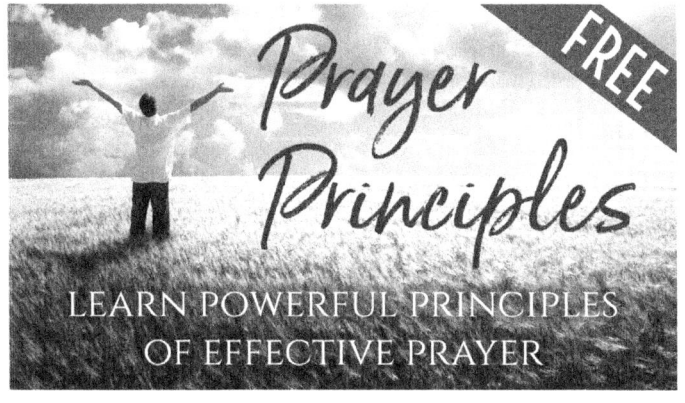

Go to JesusChrist.uk to subscribe

The *Prayer Principles Teaching Series* is a regular bite-size teaching newsletter designed to equip you to pray more effectively, and to know God in a deeper and more satisfying way.

You will **learn spiritual keys and practical principles** that you can actually use in your own passionate pursuit of God and His purpose for your life. The easy-to-digest lessons are designed to drive your heart to delight in prayer like never before.

As well as free books, videos & anointed training in proven pathways to the Father's presence you will receive teaching on…

• The Privilege of Prayer

• The Spirit of Prayer

• Passion and Prayer

• Different Kinds of Prayer

• Praying in the Spirit

• Speaking In Tongues

• Inspiring stories of answered prayer

• United Prayer

• Tabernacle or Temple Prayer

• Praying the Lord's Prayer

• Fasting and Prayer

• The Prayer of Faith

• Working and Walking with God in Prayer

• Deepening Your Relationship With God Through Prayer

• Updates of new resources created to build your spirit and stir your passion for God

…and much, much more.

Join thousands of fellow prayer warriors who are already taking this journey...

Subscribe at JesusChrist.uk

Printed in Great Britain
by Amazon